DISCOVER Kansas

the light, the land, the living

DISCOVER
Kansas

the light, the land, the living

PHOTOGRAPHY AND TEXT BY GINNY WEATHERS

FOREWORD BY BILL KURTIS

Image Press / Unicorn Publishing House
Topeka, Kansas • Verona, New Jersey

My gratitude goes to Mr. Yoh Jinno
for his constant help and support
throughout the making of this book.

Printed in Japan by Dai Nippon Printing Co. Ltd.
through DNP (America), Inc.

Printing History:
   0   1   2   3   4   5   6   7   8   9
Library of Congress Cataloging in
Publication Data Main entry under title:

preface

Do you ever wonder why you have grown to love certain things? Certain ways? As a young girl, I walked with my father across our land and I remember him saying, "This land is bluestem." I could hear the pride in his voice and, even more than that, sense the oneness he felt for the land. In the rich soil, he planted roses and trees and spent the hours outdoors raising game birds. My mother, very much like him, is an accomplished horsewoman, fisherman and hunter.

Their lives, like this land, have such a feeling of freedom, I sense this freedom, as I walk in the boundless countryside on a misty day, feeling the cool moisture on my face. I touch this freedom, as my hand holds a flower alive with color. I live this freedom, as I think my own thoughts, while sitting beside a frozen lake watching eagles play in the sky.

Photography is my way of following my parents' footsteps; for I am a roaming Kansan with a camera. Seven years ago, as I peered through the lens of my first professional camera, I saw this familiar world in a whole new way. My spirit constantly begs me to keep alive the subtle, sometimes forgotten, sometimes taken-for-granted wonders that surround us. Kansas—its struggle for survival, its struggle to make itself great—is important to me. Kansans—their lives and their work—are the energy behind that great struggle. Collectively, their lives stand for one thing—the way Kansas is today. My obligation as a photographer is to reveal the fullness of Kansas.

Those who love to take photographs know the hours are never enough. Those who are drawn to photographs are glad someone, somewhere, took the time to communicate with them. It is strange how photographs are truly reflections of our soul, and it is absolutely mysterious how lifelong experiences can be conveyed in a single photograph.

It is because of my feeling for Kansas and its people that this book exists.

Ginny Weathers
Topeka, Kansas, 1983

foreword

Several years back I wanted my children to experience the Kansas prairie as I had known it, or at least as I imagined it through the natural haze that grows over memories with the passage of time.

We pitched camp beside a pond on the state historical site where Laura Ingalls Wilder wrote the book, *Little House On the Prairie*, sixteen miles west of Independence.

It was summer. The overhead sun shimmered off the pond with metallic fury. Flat rocks at the water's edge were hot as frying pans and the tall buffalo grass stood motionless in air so stifling it seemed to take the sound out of the afternoon, as if every living thing had been muted by the heat.

As the children fished and skipped rocks across the water I began to gauge the day by the colors of the big sky, white-hot at mid-day, turning a light yellow and blue toward late afternoon. And when the sun touched the tree-line making silhouettes out of the hay-balers in the distant meadow, the sky ran the spectrum of a prism.

With darkness, the prairie started to change. What had been silent and burnt was coming to life. The crickets spoke first from weeds near the fresh water spring that filled the pond, soon joined by bullfrogs, half in and half out of the water. Coyotes on the hunt broke into the dissonant chorus with an occasional solo and cattle conversed in low bass moans that reverberated across the pastures.

The prairie's difficult survival test that afternoon had received a respite.

It was a fascinating but alien world. Most of my generation had been drawn away from the Kansas prairie to jobs which did not depend on the land and we had lost our bond. Worse, we knew little of the people who broke the virgin sod or drilled the first oil wells, those who platted the streets we call home.

They were our heritage, courageous souls who moved across the heartland armed only with the confidence that hard work invested wisely would produce a good life, hard work and prayer, for they also realized that much of their destiny was out of their hands.

If the heavens were friendly, their fields would be full. If they weren't, well, at least disappointment was equally distributed. Ethnic differences were quickly lost in the unforgiving crucible of nature.

Most of the virgin meadows have gone. We may have lost our ancestor's close communion with the land, but if we study the prairie lifestyle we can find a Kansas legacy that has passed from one family to the next. Its traces are still evident in the faces that have watched the seasons change, who have known the gamble of making a living on the land but have learned that while the prairie tests its inhabitants harshly, it also rewards. They know that for every harsh and colorless winter there will be golden coreopsis surrounding the summer's wheat.

Those lessons almost passed with that noisy prairie night until I saw Ginny Weathers' photographs and discovered that she also possessed the Kansas legacy. She has captured the light which stalks the land, sometimes harsh, often in delicate veils as it transforms a flat terrain into an impressionist's canvas. In a single picture, she gives us a bridge between past and present, a chronicle for those who live on the prairie and a marvelous guide for those who want to Discover Kansas.

Bill Kurtis

For my children, Marcie and Brady
And for my mother, Kathleen A. Costelow.

the light, the land, the living

the light

The sun had just risen;
It came slowly—almost as if it appeared ray by ray.
First I noticed it lit up the side of the barn,
Then the wildflowers appeared to sparkle before me.
I was alone . . .
Yet I was a part of a whole,
A oneness with the earth, the flowers and the light.

Kansas is...
Worn, weather-beaten barns telling a story of another time.

It was a beautiful fun day.
I wandered aimlessly through the Flint Hills;
Each curve brought a new visual surprise.

It was raining.
Kansas was showing off her colors.
The hills were painted with shades of deep greens,
lemon yellows and burnt umbers.
The brown tree trunks looked black . . .
Contrasts were everywhere.

I couldn't see enough.
It was almost as if I could breathe in the beauty of the
Kansas countryside.

It was all here—
Old wheel-shaped bridges, striped green hills, lonely
trees, antique stone barns and Stetson-hatted
cowboys with yellow slickers.

the land

Kansas is . . .
Country farm atmosphere,
Side roads,
Hawks riding the currents,
Friendly people and
Land reflected in a farmer's face.

It was another world,
All green and golden,
Leaves all over the ground,
Fallen logs,
Little streams;
It was quiet, peaceful.

A wildflower
Dancing in the wind,
Light sparkling through its petals,
Waiting there to spread the joy of its existence.

With winter's slow death,
Spring is born.

The never ending circle of nature and man, springing
from life's seed.
The seed, like one thought, bursts forth to breed new
thoughts, new beauty, new flowers.

It was a whole new world—
Confusing at first;
All my landmarks were covered with snow.
I plodded down a forest road.
The only tracks in front of me were deer, rabbits and
something small, possibly a bird.

Snow was thick, everywhere.
It was an incredible experience.
My senses were overwhelmed with a totally fresh creation.
A realm I had never really experienced.

How could this have happened?
The brown farm pond now resembled a kingdom fit for
a fairy princess.
The snow glistened with billions of diamonds reflected
by the sun.
Everywhere I turned I saw something beautiful.

I walked on through the trees;
A still unfrozen stream curved its way gracefully through
this sparkling wonderland.
A bird whirred past me several times, angry I had entered
his domain.

I finished my work and left.
I felt my presence was an intrusion.

The farmer put off cutting his field till sunset so
I could photograph it.
What a wonderful gift he gave to me.

A fallen leaf
A thing of beauty
Lying there so simply
Nature's gift for those willing to see.

the living

I stopped at a farmhouse.
An old man came out, happy for company. His face
reflected many hours, days, years of being in the open
riding his tractor. He gave me a tour of his place,
explaining with pride exactly when everything was built
and how much it cost.
He was great. His farm was great.

It was a photographer's dream—old wagons and old wagon
wheels, anything and everything.

The morning fog came slowly in
Settling unnoticed on leaves, blades of grass
and the spider's web.
Creating a new phenomenon,
A new beauty,
A necklace,
A work of art.

There is so much beauty in Kansas,
Seeing a farmer's lined face,
A cowboy's roughened hands,
A child's inquiring look,
The unfolding beauty of a young girl,
A touch,
A feeling,
A depth beyond the heart.

Somehow, I liked it.
I felt at home here.
The old lace curtains,
The sun shining through,
There was warmth here.

The room was old.
The wallpaper belonged to a different time.
I wanted to walk over and touch it.
The bed was high and the furniture, heavy.

Kansas is . . .
Listening to the crickets at night,
Watching the Miller's climb the screen,
Peace in a porch swing and
Taking rides in the country.

Traveling from one community to another, seeing the proud old homes, the old stores, the beautiful stone churches and visiting with the people brings a feeling of pride in our state.

Kansas is . . .
Wildflowers bursting forth in the spring,
Catching the wind in your sails,
Summer ending with an explosion of golds, ochers,
peach, emeralds, jades and glorious golden browns.
Taking a long drink from the clear water bubbling up
from the ground.
Clear, bright fresh air.

Protected in the mare is her treasure of wealth.

It was a heron rookery,
A small town of birds,
Nest upon nest,
Each holding two or three large baby herons,
They squawked and squawked.
It was a confused uproar,
Each one feeling the need to express himself.
Nothing could be heard over the din of these talkative
birds.

One would jump up and flap his wings, then another
would follow suit.
It was a comical show.
They were trying to fly with nose-dives, loops, and,
sometimes,
A crash landing.

They would fly from nest to nest slowly building strength
in their wings.
Then the day finally came. The testing was over.

They flapped their wings, launched into the air, caught
the current and flew with unbounded freedom.

I once heard a Kansan say, "I hope no one else finds out about Kansas."

appendix

the light

2. Golden wheat heads: the "Wheat State" where vast wheat fields leave a visual impression capable of exciting the great artists of our time.

5. Sunflower: adopted by the legislature as the official state flower in 1903.

12., 13. Sunset: looking west toward Indian Hills Road, west of Topeka in Shawnee county.

14. Barn: is located at the Topeka Round-Up Club west of the city.

15. Windmill: one of the many sentinels that dot the Kansas countryside located a few miles west of Buhler in Reno county.

16. Boats: sunset beautifully silhouettes the sailboats at Lake Perry. The Perry Dam and a large portion of the lake itself are located on the old Delaware Indian Reservation, 17 miles northeast of Topeka.

17. River: Kansas River named for the Kansa or Kaw tribe of Indians which lived on its banks. Kansa or Kansas is a Siouan word which means Wind People or People of the Wind. The view of the river can be seen from the bridge south of Rossville.

18., 19. River: south of Wamego the Kansas River turns golden at sunset.

20., 21. Clouds: build over Cheyenne Bottoms near Great Bend.

22. Grasses: sunlight turns these beautiful Kansas grasses to a warm golden brown.

23. Grasses: fall grasses in northern Pottawatomie county.

24. Lesser Sandhill Cranes: leaving the rivers at sunrise.

25. Power stations: the setting sun showing off the abundantly available power of Kansas. This electricity comes from coal-fired power plants. The image is of the Auburn substation west of Topeka.

26. Water lilies; photographed at Gage Park in Topeka have the simplicity and beauty of oriental art.

27. Goat's Beard: looking like a burst of fireworks the weed commonly called Goat's beard starts to bloom in early June throughout Kansas.

29. Lake Shawnee: the hush of winter descends on Lake Shawnee in Topeka making it a remote place of solitude.

30. Barn: ten miles north of Hutchinson along highway 61 can be seen an old barn and a windmill reminding us of the families who lived through dust, winds and rains.

31. Sailboat: Lake Sherwood in Shawnee county is just one of the many lakes in Kansas used for summer fun and recreation.

32., 33. Castle Rock: located in Gove county.

35. Flint Hills: near I-70 and Manhattan.

36., 37. Windmill: another day is starting in Reno county with the sun just beginning to come up behind the hill.

the land

40., 41. Farm field: the land north of the Kaw River is some of the state's richest farmland.

42. Daisies: south of Maple Hill on highway 30 looking west.

43. Pond: surrounded by Kansas wildflowers is alongside Highway 61 west of Buhler.

44. Flint Hills: early morning east of St. Marys.

45. Breidenthal Forest: owned by Kansas University, south of Lawrence, is the sight of many trees including ash, black walnut, elm, hickory, maple, locust, oak, sycamore and willow.

46. Combine: harvesting in central Kansas.

47. Wheat: one of the major crops grown in rich farmland.

48., 49. Finger Coreopsis: bloom in Kansas in late July and August.

50. Purple Poppy Mallow: in the spring wildflowers are everywhere especially the Purple Poppy Mallow found in Kiowa county.

51. Sweet Rocket: a member of the mustard family blooming north of Council Grove on highway 177.

52. Sunflowers: north of Hutchinson.

53. Grasses: Riley county near Plaine was the scene for the photograph of the fall hills and grasses.

54., 55. Fence (top): the graphic quality of the scene in Shawnee county reflects the many views of Kansas.

54. Canadian geese (bottom): lay over in Kansas to feed and regain strength while waiting for winter to break before traveling north.

55. Red barn: the snow created an all-white world except for the red barn west of Dover on K-4 highway.

56. Pine: close-up views of Kansas are spectacular.

57. Ice on grasses: ice storms bring even more breathtaking beauty to Kansas.

59. Stream: part of the Shunganunga Creek below the dam at Lake Sherwood in Shawnee county.

60. Snow: Kansas farmland, one mile west of Dover on K-4, takes on a quieter beauty in winter.

61. Snow: below the dam at Lake Sherwood in Shawnee county.

62. Trees: Kansas is a land of contrasts as brought out by this starkly quiet scene at Lake Sherwood, southwest of Topeka.

63. Waterfall: when the spring snows melt, the spillway at Lake Wabaunsee turns into a beautiful waterfall.

64. Ducks: settling down for the night on a Kansas lake.

65. Trees: the beautiful stark quality of this image is a result of flooding by the Arkansas River near Buhler in Reno county.

66. Wheat: near Cedar Point in Chase county, the wheat was just beginning to turn to a golden yellow.

67. Tree: silhouetted against a typically beautiful Kansas sunset. The tree is located south of Manhattan in Geary county.

68. Combine: Kenneth Kerwin cutting his wheat near Delia.

69. Country road: near Plaine in Riley county.

70. Barn: located at the Moore Ranch, south of Mullinville in Kiowa county.

71. Sheep (top): farm on Wanamaker Road in Topeka.

71. Door knob (middle): photographed in Osage county.

71. Knob and barn door (bottom): a glimpse of yesterday, found on an old barn in Osage county.

72. Maple leaf: found north of Leavenworth.

73. Jonquil: Kansas shows off her colors with beautiful flowering trees, jonquils, tulips and many other spring flowers.

74., 75. Wheat field: located north of Great Bend in Barton county.

the living

78., 79. Horses: mare and foul are located on the Moore Ranch in Kiowa county.

80. Loyce Bert Jernigan: ninety-years-old, owns and operates a 1,000 acre farm south of Osage City.

81. Brady Weathers: thirteen-years-old lives in Topeka.

82. Joe Moore: son of Ray Moore helps his father operate the longhorn steer operation at the Moore Ranch south of Mullinville in Kiowa county.

83. Wagon: it's almost an escape into the history of Kansas, however, the wagon is still put to good use on the farm south of Osage City in Osage county.

84., 85. Stone barn: built by Mell and Sam Sjogren's father. One of the barns was destroyed by a·tornado in 1966. Pictured is 85-year-old Sam Sjogren.

86. Barn interior: The Topeka Round-Up Club west of Topeka in Shawnee county.

87. Spider's web: hanging on a bush above a stream in northeastern Kansas.

88. Marcie Weathers: eighteen-years-old lives in Topeka.

89. Cats: at The Topeka Round-Up Club west of Topeka in Shawnee county.

90. Willia May Woosypiti: Wichita in Sedgwick county.

91. Ray Moore: owner of the Moore Ranch south of Mullinville in Kiowa county.

92. The Brookville Hotel: beautiful historic hotel with authentic antique furniture located in Brookville west of Salina on highway 140.

93. Brookville Hotel: another example of the nostalgic quality of the hotel located in Brookville west of Salina on highway 140.

94. Eisenhower Family Home: the Eisenhower Center in Abilene is among the nation's leading tourist attractions.

95. The Brookville Hotel: hallway in Brookville Hotel. The hotel is known for its beautiful antiques and fine food.

96. Mark and Joyce Meers: enjoying Gage Park in Topeka.

97. Amelia Earheart home: the American aviatrix was born in this lovely frame house in Atchison. Atchison is well known for its elegantly restored Victorian mansions.

98. The Main Post Chapel: located Fort Riley. Fort Riley is one of the oldest established military posts west of the Mississippi River.

99. Yoder Mennonite Church: located in Yoder in Reno county.

100., 101. Amish buggy: photographed north of Yoder in Reno county.

102. Fort Larned: seven miles west of Larned, established in 1859 to protect travelers and commerce on the Santa Fe Trail.

103. Swedish Pavilion: built in Sweden for the 1904 World's Fair as an example of a Swedish manor house and later given to Bethany College who then presented it to the city of Lindsborg.

104., 105. Washburn University Observatory and skyline of Topeka: Washburn University, founded in 1865, has grown with the capital city and is the focus of the community educational and cultural interests.

106., 107. Sailrider: on Lake Sherwood west of Topeka.

108., 109. Horses: traveling through Kansas on a snowy day there are many beautiful sights including these horses running through the snowy powder on Green Post Farm, one mile south of Holton in Jackson county.

110. Cows: the image, photographed north of Plainville, shows the picturesque beauty of Kansas.

111. Horse: 'Wielka Kreana', an Arabian mare, on the Serenata Farms on highway 40 at Big Springs east of Topeka.

112. Horse: located on Wanamaker Road in Topeka.

113. Mare and foul: the Moore Ranch south of Mullinville in Kiowa county.

114. Great Blue Herons: nesting at Lake Perry east of Topeka.

116., 117. Great Blue Heron: the herons migrate to the lake areas in early spring in Kansas. The heron was photographed at Lake Perry in March.

118. Duck (top): photographed at Lake Sherwood west of Topeka.

118. Pelicans (bottom): large flocks of pelicans are found at Cheyenne Bottoms.

119. Great Blue Heron (top): found fishing early morning at Lake Sherwood.

120., 121. Lesser Sandhill Cranes: fly over Kansas heading for their feeding grounds near the Platte River in Nebraska.

122. Bird (top): the Tropical Rain Forest at Gage Park features lush tropical vegetation and birds in free flight.

122. Black Crown Night Heron (bottom): located at Cheyenne Bottoms, a 19,000-acre wildlife refuge, the largest free public shooting area in the U.S. and provides a place for excellent migratory bird watching.

123. American Bald Eagle: moves into the Lake Perry area in the winter and leaves for the northern States by March or April.

124., 125. Birds: Cheyenne Bottoms in Barton county is the stopover feeding ground for thousands of waterfowl.

128. Windmill: lonely windmill and a beautiful sunset looking west toward Medora in Reno county are typical of the quiet Kansas countryside.